WAR MACHINES
WARSHIPS

Simon Adams

A+

Smart Apple Media

IN ASSOCIATION WITH

IMPERIAL WAR
MUSEUM

Smart Apple Media is published by Black Rabbit Books
P.O. Box 3263, Mankato, Minnesota 56002

Printed in the United States

Published by arrangement with the Watts Publishing Group Ltd, London.

Library of Congress Cataloging-in-Publication Data
Adams, Simon.
     Warships / Simon Adams.
        p. cm—(Smart Apple Media. War machines)
     Includes index.
     Summary: "Describes several models of battleships and submarines used in World War I and World War II, including specifications and statistics"—Provided by publisher.
        ISBN 978-1-59920-225-9
        1. Warships—History—Juvenile literature. I. Title.
V750.A23 2009
940.4'59—dc22

                                                    2007045461

Editor: Sarah Ridley
Editor-in-chief: John C. Miles
Designer: Jason Billin
Art director: Jonathan Hair

A note on sources used for this book: The specifications and statistics in this book are compiled from various sources and amended to include information held by the Imperial War Museum.

A note on weights in this book: The ton weights given for the displacement or weight of ships in this book are long tons, equal to 2,240 pounds. Weights of ships are traditionally expressed in long tons.

A note on speeds in this book: The speed of a ship is given in knots. A knot is one nautical mile per hour. A nautical mile is 1.15 statute miles.

Picture credits:
All images copyright © Imperial War Museum EXCEPT Bettmann/Corbis: 17t, 20, 21t. Corbis: 20-21 background. The Mariners' Museum/Corbis: 21b.

IWM copyright images: cover t Q80706, bl HU50897, bm Q53022, br Q39216; title page HU50748; p4 Q21183; p5 HU50748; p6 Q38891, p7t Q38884, p7b Q38881; pp8-9 bg Q38705, p8 Q21184, 9t SP3127, 9b Q41434; p10 Q80706, p11 Q22361; p12 Q22719, p13 Q22725; p 14 Q39216, p15 Q21382; p16 Q19305; pp18-19 bg Q23862, p18 Q20389, p19t Q53022, p19b Q53013; pp22-23 bg A25664, p22 A18642, p23 A20687; pp24-25 bg GM4510, p24 HU50841, p25 A9821; pp26-27bg HU50744, p26 HU50926, p27t HU50897, p27b HU50822; p28 MH4494, p29 NYF68821; pp30-31bg BU4556.

9 8 7 6 5 4 3 2

Contents

Introduction

The 20th century was a great age of warships. Powerful ships built of steel, powered by steam, and equipped with massive guns ruled the seas, while submarines lurked below the surface ready to destroy enemy ships with torpedoes (underwater missiles).

Sea Battles

The most powerful navies in the world—the British and German in World War I (1914–18); the British, German, United States (U.S.), and Japanese in World War II (1939–45)—clashed in great battles at sea. The naval battles of World War I rarely achieved a decisive result, while those in World War II decided the war in both the Pacific and the Atlantic oceans. Some of these battles were spectacular. The Battle of the Coral Sea, fought between U.S. and the Japanese in 1942, was the first aircraft carrier battle in history. It took place over such a huge area that the fleets never met—only their aircraft made contact.

About This Book

This book includes warships and submarines from both world wars and the major navies. Their statistics, engines, armor, and guns are all described, as well as something about their history and naval service. All the ships are called "she," as that is the custom at sea. There is a glossary of difficult words on page 30.

HMS
Formidable

HMS *Formidable* **holds the unfortunate distinction of being the first British battleship to be sunk during World War I.**

This aged battleship, which gave her name to a class of eight warships, was on patrol in the English Channel when a German U-boat torpedoed her. She sank quickly in bad weather with the loss of 547 of her 780-man crew.

Formidable Battleships

HMS *Formidable* was the first of eight Formidable-class battleships that came into service between 1901 and 1904. At the time, they were technically advanced, with steel armor and construction, revolving gun turrets and triple-expansion steam engines. However, the introduction of faster and more efficient torpedoes made these ships vulnerable to torpedo attack, and they were replaced by the more powerfully armed Dreadnought-class (*see* pages 8–9).

HMS Formidable *was a state-of-the-art warship when launched, but became vulnerable to torpedo attack later.*

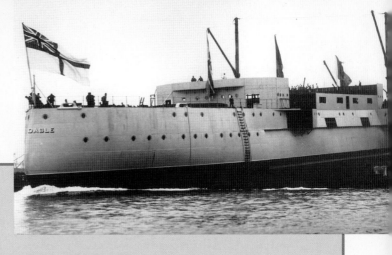

FACT FILE

★ Two of the eight Formidable-class battleships—*Formidable* and *Irresistible*—were both sunk in 1915. HMS *Bulwark* suffered an internal explosion while in harbor in Nov. 1914 that killed all but 12 of her 750-man crew. The other five battleships—*Implacable, London, Venerable, Queen,* and *Prince of Wales*—were all broken up or sold for scrap.

▲ *HMS* Formidable *was launched stern first from her shipyard.*

ARMS & ARMOR

Guns	Four 12-in (30-cm) guns
	Twelve 6-in (15-cm) guns
	Sixteen 12-pdr (5.4-kg) guns
	Six 3-pdr (1.4-kg) guns
	Two machine guns
Torpedo tubes	Four 18-in (45-cm) tubes
Armor	Hull: 9 in (23 cm)
	Decks: 3 in (7.5 cm)
	Gun turrets: 10 in (25 cm)
	Barbettes: 12 in (30 cm)

SPECS & STATS

Launched	Portsmouth, England, November 17, 1898
Crew	780
Displacement	15,800 tons (16,053 t)
Length	431.7 ft (131 m)
Beam	75 ft (23 m)
Draft	26.7 ft (8.2 m)
Speed	18 knots (33 km/h)
Engines	Two 15,500 hp marine piston engines

▶ *The crew of HMS* Formidable *lines the decks while she slowly cruises in harbor.*

HMS *Dreadnought*

HMS *Dreadnought* was truly one of the most revolutionary battleships of all time.

Her name became a general word for all modern battleships, while the older ships she replaced became known as "pre-dreadnoughts." HMS *Dreadnought* triggered a new major naval arms race between Britain and Germany in the years leading up to World War I, yet she herself soon became out of date as newer ships outpaced her.

Best Battleship

Prior to the *Dreadnought*, battleships were armed with a mix of guns, a few large ones and many smaller weapons. HMS *Dreadnought* had a large battery of 10 same-size big guns. These allowed her to accurately outgun every other warship afloat. She was also the first large warship to be powered by steam turbines. These were a revolutionary new type of marine engine developed by Sir Charles Parsons. The turbine engines made *Dreadnought*s the fastest battleships in the world at that time.

▼ *Afloat and equipped, HMS* Dreadnought *was the most powerful warship of her age.*

SPECS & STATS

Launched	February 10, 1906
Crew	695–773
Displacement	18,420 tons (18,715 t)
Length	527 ft (160 m)
Beam	82 ft (25 m)
Draft	26 ft (8 m)
Speed	21 knots (39 km/h)
Engines	Four 22,500 hp steam turbines

▲ HMS Dreadnought *in dry dock undergoing a refit.*

FACT FILE

★ The only action HMS *Dreadnought* saw in World War I took place on March 18, 1915, when she sank German submarine U-29. She is the only battleship ever to have directly sunk a submarine.

★ In 1910 a group of the Abyssinian royal family (from what is now Ethiopia) toured the ship. In fact the "royals" were a group of hoaxers, including the novelist Virginia Woolf, dressed in disguise with their faces painted black.

▼ *The launch of* HMS Dreadnought *(background) in 1906.*

ARMS & ARMOR

Guns	Ten 12-in (30-cm) main guns
	Twenty-four 12-pdr (5.4-kg) guns
Torpedo tubes	Five 18-in (45-cm) tubes
Armor	Hull: 4–11 in (100–280 mm)
	Deck: up to 3 in (75 mm)
	Conning tower: 11 in (280 mm)
	Gun turrets: 11 in (280 mm)
	Barbettes: up to 8 in (200 mm)

SMS
Scharnhorst

SMS *Scharnhorst*—like SMS *Emden* (*see* **pages 12–13**)—formed part of the German East Asia Squadron based at the German colony of Tsingtao on the Chinese coast.

Vice-Admiral Maximilian Graf von Spee, in charge of the squadron, realized that the colony would be attacked when World War I broke out in August 1914. So he gave orders for the fleet to sail across the Pacific and into the Atlantic Ocean. Five ships, including his flagship, the *Scharnhorst*, sank two British cruisers off the coast of Chile. They then rounded Cape Horn to attack the Falkland Islands to get more coal for their engines.

ARMS & ARMOR

Guns	Eight 8.2-in (21-cm) guns
	Six 5.9-in (15-cm) guns
	Eighteen 3.45-in (88-mm) guns
Torpedo tubes	Four 18 in (45 cm) tubes
Armor	Hull: 4 to 6 in (10 to 12 cm)
	Turrets: 6 in (15 cm)

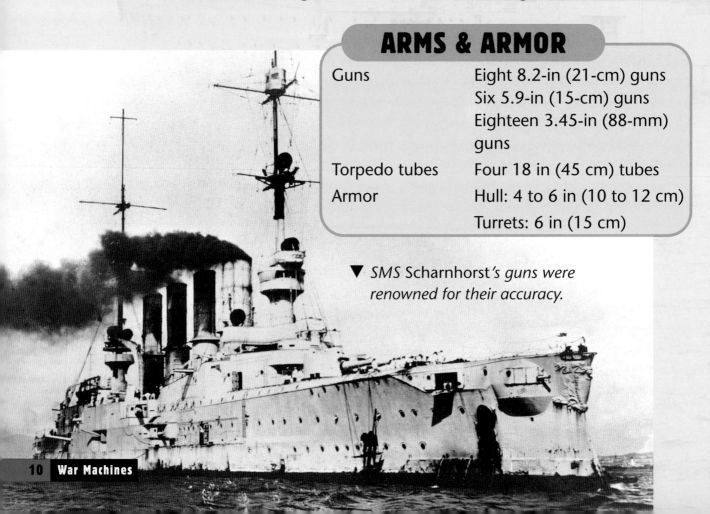

▼ *SMS* Scharnhorst*'s guns were renowned for their accuracy.*

Disaster Strikes

However, the German squadron did not realize that a larger and stronger British squadron had just arrived at the Islands. The Germans stood no chance when the two squadrons met on December 8, 1914. The *Scharnhorst* sank with all crew lost. Three other ships also sank. The *Dresden* escaped, only to be sunk off Chile three months later.

SPECS & STATS

Launched	Hamburg, Germany, March 26, 1906
Crew	764
Displacement	11,616 tons (11,800 t)
Length	474.7 ft (144.6 m)
Beam	71 ft (21.6 m)
Draught	27.5 ft (8.4 m)
Speed	22.7 knots (42 km/h)
Engines	Eighteen coal-fired boilers
	Three 27,759 hp triple expansion piston engines

▼ *Four large funnels allowed smoke from the coal-fired boilers to escape.*

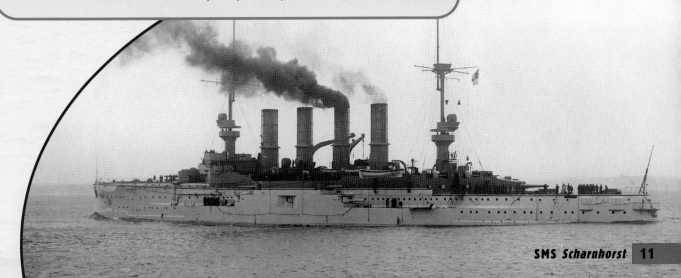

SMS *Emden*

When World War I broke out in August 1914, the German light cruiser *Emden* was at sea off the coast of China.

Her captain, Karl von Müller, then sailed her into the Indian Ocean to attack British and Allied ships. In September 1914, she captured and sank 15 British ships. She later shelled the British ports of Madras in India and Penang in Malaya (now Malaysia), where she sank a Russian cruiser before attacking ships across the Indian Ocean.

Hunting the *Emden*

By now, 60 Allied warships were searching for the *Emden*, which was tracked down on November 9, 1914, by HMAS *Sydney* of the Royal Australian Navy in the Cocos (Keeling) Islands northwest of Australia. *Emden* was no match for the *Sydney* and was soon overpowered. Her captain beached her to prevent her from sinking. After the crew surrendered, the *Emden* was destroyed.

▼ SMS Emden *was beached on North Keeling Island to prevent her from sinking.*

A German raiding party in the Cocos (Keeling) Islands hurriedly returning to SMS Emden *after having received news that HMAS* Sydney *was on her way to attack their ship.*

SPECS & STATS

Launched	26 May 1908, Danzig, Germany
Crew	360
Displacement	3,364 tons (3,418 t)
Length	387 ft (118 m)
Beam	44 ft (13.4 m)
Draft	17.4 ft (5.3 m)
Speed	23 knots (44 km/h)
Engines	Twelve coal-fired boilers Two 16,000 hp 3-cylinder triple expansion reciprocating steam engines

FACT FILE

★ In October 1914, SMS *Emden* shelled a customs boat off the coast of Malaya. When Müller realized the boat was unarmed, *Emden* ceased fire and sent an apology for having attacked a defenseless vessel.

★ SMS *Emden* was the last piston-engined warship in the German navy. Her sister ship, *Dresden*, was equipped with steam turbines, as were all later ships.

HMS *Indefatigable*

On May 31, 1916 the battle cruiser HMS *Indefatigable* took part in the most important naval battle of World War I, fought in the North Sea off Jutland in Denmark.

The British Grand Fleet engaged the German High Seas Fleet, the British losing 14 warships, the German 10 warships. The numbers might suggest otherwise, but the British actually won the battle, as the German fleet returned to port and remained there for the rest of the war.

▼ *In 1911, HMS* Indefatigable *joined other British warships for a naval review off Spithead, England.*

Sinking the *Indefatigable*

At 6:33 p.m., the SMS *Von der Tann* hit HMS *Indefatigable* during a long-range gunnery duel. Two shells hit the "X" magazine (ammunition storage) at the stern of the ship. It then exploded, causing the ship to sink at the stern.

FACT FILE

★ A battle cruiser is a ship midway in size between a cruiser and a battleship. It saved weight by having less armor than a battleship, allowing more powerful engines to be fitted.

More shells then hit the forward "A" gun turret. Although the turret had fireproof anti-flash doors, they had been left open to improve the rate of gunfire. The blaze caused by the shell hits soon spread to the forward magazine, causing a massive explosion that sank the ship. All but four of the crew died.

SPECS & STATS

Launched	Devonport, England, October 28, 1909
Crew	800
Displacement	18,750 tons (19,050 t)
Length	578 ft (177 m)
Beam	79.5 ft (24.5 m)
Draft	27 ft (8 m)
Speed	25.8 knots (48 km/h)
Engines	Thirty-two boilers Four 43,000 hp steam turbines

ARMS & ARMOR

Guns	Eight 12-in (30-cm) guns, Sixteen 4-in (10-cm) guns Four 3-pdr 1-in (26-mm) guns Two 3-in (7.6-cm) antiaircraft guns fitted in 1915
Torpedo tubes	Three 18-in (45-cm) tubes
Armor	Hull: 4–8 in (10–20 cm) Decks: 3 in (7.5 cm) Gun turrets: 10 in (25 cm), Barbettes: 7 in (17.5 cm)

▼ *HMS* Indefatigable *had long, sleek lines and a low profile.*

SMS *Seydlitz*

The SMS *Seydlitz* was the most advanced battle cruiser in the German navy when she was built. She was also unique in design, as she was a one-off ship based on an older design.

The *Seydlitz* saw action at the Battle of Dogger Bank in the North Sea in 1915, when a British shell destroyed two rear gun turrets, and again at the Battle of Jutland in 1916. Damaged in that action, she was repaired and back in service by November 1916.

FACT FILE

★ The *Seydlitz* survived more damage than any other German warship during World War I.

★ The motto of the *Seydlitz* was "Always forward."

▲ *The unique SMS* Seydlitz, *the only ship of her class.*

ARMS & ARMOR

Guns	Ten 11.2-in (284-mm) guns
	Twelve 5.9-in (150-mm) guns
	Twelve 3.45-in (88-mm) guns
Torpedo tubes	Four 20 in (50 cm)
Armor	Hull: 4 to 11 in (10 to 27.5 cm)

SPECS & STATS

Launched	Hamburg, Germany, March 30, 1912
Crew	1,068
Displacement	24,594 tons (24,990 t)
Length	658 ft (200.5 m)
Beam	93.5 ft (28.5 m)
Draft	27 ft (30.3 m)
Speed	26.5 knots (49 km/h)
Engines	Four 63,000 hp steam turbines

▲ *SMS* Seydlitz *and the rest of the German fleet were deliberately sunk in June 1919 to prevent the ships from falling into British hands.*

The End of the German Fleet

After the defeat of Germany in 1918, *Seydlitz* and the remaining 74 ships of the German High Seas Fleet sailed to Scapa Flow in the Orkney Islands, north of Scotland, to await a decision about their future. On June 21, 1919, while the British fleet was out at sea, the German officer in command at Scapa Flow gave orders for all the German ships to be scuttled (deliberately sunk) to prevent their falling into British hands. *Seydlitz* remained on the seafloor until she was salvaged in 1928 and then scrapped.

U-35

U-35 was one of the most successful German submarines of World War I.

In 25 patrols from January 1915 until November 1918, she sank 224 merchant ships and two gunboats. For most of the war, U-35 was based at the Austrian naval base of Cattaro on the Adriatic. Austria–Hungary fought with Germany in World War I.

A fleet of U-boats lies in harbor awaiting orders.

Record

Under Lothar von Arnauld de la Periere, captain from November 1915 until March 1918, U-35 sailed on 15 missions and sank 195 merchant ships with a total of 446,708 tons (453,855 t). She also sank a British and a French gunboat. Her patrol from July 26, 1916 to August 20, 1916, was the most successful patrol of any submarine in either world war. A total of 54 merchant ships totaling 90,350 tons (91,796 t) were sunk in just 26 days, more than two a day! At the end of the war in 1918, U-35 was transferred to Britain and docked in England until she was broken up in 1920.

▲ *Some of the crew of U-35 watch from the conning tower.*

SPECS & STATS

Launched	Kiel, Germany, April 18, 1914
Crew	35
Displacement	971 tons (987 t)
Overall length	212 ft (64.7 m)
Overall beam	20.7 ft (6.32 m)
Height	25.2 ft (7.68 m)
Draft	11.7 ft (3.56 m)
Surface speed	16.4 knots (30.3 km/h)
Engine	Diesel engine generating 1,850 hp on the surface Electric engine generating 1,200 hp when submerged

FACT FILE

★ U-35 was one of 11 submarines in the Type U-31 (*Mittle–U*, "middle-size") class built at the Germaniawerft shipyard in Kiel between 1912 and 1915. The 11 subs were numbered U-31 to U-41.

★ Captain de la Periere was famous for allowing the crew of enemy merchant ships to board their lifeboats and for giving them directions to the nearest port before sinking their ships.

▼ *In dock in May 1917, U-35 stocks up with supplies for her next mission.*

ARMS & ARMOR

Torpedo tubes	Two in bow, two in stern, carrying six torpedoes
Deck gun	4.1 in (105 mm) with 300 rounds

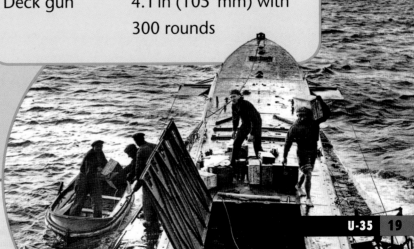

USS *Enterprise*

USS *Enterprise* (CV-6)—(the aircraft carrier, not the spacecraft!)—was the sixth aircraft carrier of the U.S. Navy and the seventh U.S. Navy ship to bear this name.

She was one of three Yorktown-class aircraft carriers, along with USS *Yorktown* and USS *Hornet*, and was one of only three aircraft carriers built before World War II to survive the war. She was nicknamed the "Big E" because of her size.

▼ *Assisted by a tug, USS* Enterprise *steams into New York harbor.*

FACT FILE

★ USS *Enterprise* was vulnerable to torpedo attack. During a refit in 1942, the ship was given an anti-torpedo blister (armored bulge) to improve her underwater protection.

★ On May 14, 1945 the ship was put out of action when a Japanese *kamikaze* suicide pilot crashed into the forward aircraft elevator and damaged the hangar deck.

ARMS & ARMOR (as built)

Guns	Eight 5-in (127-mm) guns
	Sixteen 1.1-in (28-mm) antiaircraft guns
	Twenty-four .5-in (13-mm) machine guns
Aircraft	Ninety aircraft
	Three elevators up to flight deck
	One flight-deck hydraulic catapult
	Two hangar-deck hydraulic catapults
Armor	Hull: 2.5 to 4 in (64 to 100 mm)
	Deck, bulkheads, conning tower: 4 in (10 cm)

▲ Some of her 90 aircraft wait on deck to take off for action.

Action in the Pacific

When the Japanese attacked the U.S. naval base at Pearl Harbor on December 7, 1941, USS *Enterprise* was out at sea. Her planes flew into action in defense of the base. Six were shot down by the Japanese, although one later sank a Japanese submarine. From then on, the *Enterprise* served in all the major battles against Japan in the Pacific Ocean and earned 20 battle stars, the most for any U.S. warship in World War II.

▼ Looking up at the two hangar deck hydraulic catapults.

SPECS & STATS (as built)

Launched	Newport News, Virginia, October 3, 1936
Crew	2,072
Displacement	25,500 tons (25,908 t)
Length	809.5 ft (246.7 m)
Beam	109.5 ft (33.4 m)
Draft	26 ft (7.9 m)
Speed	32.5 knots (60.2 km/h)
Engines	Nine boilers
	Four 120,000 hp geared steam turbines

HMS *Belfast*

▼ The hull of HMS Belfast was camouflaged to confuse the enemy.

HMS *Belfast* was one of 10 Town-class cruisers of the Royal Navy.

She was launched in Belfast, Northern Ireland, on St. Patrick's Day, March 17, 1938. She saw service in World War II and the Korean War (1950–53). From 1959–62, she operated in the Far East. Since 1971, she has been moored on the River Thames in London. In 1978, she became part of the Imperial War Museum.

World War II Action

HMS *Belfast* took part in the naval blockade of Germany in 1939, but was seriously damaged by a mine in November 1939 and spent almost three years undergoing major repairs. She returned to service in November 1942 and escorted Arctic convoys to Russia, taking part in operations against the German warships *Scharnhorst* and *Tirpitz*. In June 1944, HMS *Belfast* supported the British and Canadian assaults on Gold and Juno beaches as part of the D-Day landings in Normandy. She was in action for the next five weeks, bombarding German positions ahead of the advancing Allies.

FACT FILE

★ HMS *Belfast* was designed to carry her 6-in (152-mm) guns in batteries of four. These proved to be difficult to construct, so each battery was reduced to three guns. The weight saved was used to improve the ship's armor and antiaircraft defenses.

★ The original cost of the ship was $4,357,092, of which $152,583 was for the guns and $135,279 for the aircraft.

▲ *The extreme cold of the Arctic Ocean often coated the guns and other equipment on board with ice.*

ARMS & ARMOR

Guns	Twelve 6-in (152-mm) guns Eight 4-in (100-mm) guns
Antiaircraft guns	Twelve Bofors 1.5-in (40-mm) guns
Torpedo tubes	Two 21-in (53-cm) tubes
Aircraft	Two Supermarine Walrus reconnaissance seaplanes
Armor	Hull: 4.5 in (11. 4 cm) Deck: 3 in (7.5 cm)

SPECS & STATS

Launched	Harland & Wolff Shipyard, Belfast, March 17, 1938
Crew	750
Displacement	11,553 tons (11,738 t)
Length	613.5 ft (187 m)
Beam	69 ft (21 m)
Draft	19.75 ft (6.1 m)
Speed	32 knots (59 km/h)
Engines	Four oil-fired three-drum boilers Four 80,000 hp single reduction geared steam turbines

U-48

U-48 was the most successful German submarine of World War II.

During her two years of active service, she sank 57 ships totaling 333,000 tons (338,328 t). U-48 was a Type VIIB submarine, which had great speed and agility thanks to her dual-rudder steering. She could stay on patrol for up to a month at a time, making her particularly deadly during the long-range Battle of the Atlantic against Allied merchant shipping.

International Outrage

On September 18, 1940, the U-48 sank the British liner SS *City of Benares* in the North Atlantic, killing 256 people, leaving 150 survivors, some of whom were not picked up for eight days. The ship was carrying 77 children evacuated from London to escape the German aerial bombardment of the city. The Germans had no way of knowing who was on the ship and thought it a legitimate military target. Despite this fact, the sinking caused international outrage and further damaged Germany's standing in the then-neutral U.S.

▼ *In May 1945, U-48 surrendered to* HMS Malcolm *off Gibraltar.*

▶ *Conditions were cramped in a submarine's engine room.*

FACT FILE

★ U-48 was already on patrol in the Atlantic when war started between Germany and Britain on September 3, 1939. She sank her first ship, the SS *Royal Sceptre*, two days later, and another two as she returned home on September 17th.

★ U-48 was one of 24 Type VIIB U-boats built between 1936 and 1940. Increased fuel tanks and additional armaments made them much better than the first generation Type VIIA attack U-boats.

SPECS & STATS

Launched	Kiel, Germany, March 8, 1939
Crew	44–48
Displacement	857 tons (871 t)
Overall length	218.3 ft (66.5 m)
Overall beam	20.3 ft (6.2 m)
Height	31.2 ft (9.5 m)
Draft	15.6 ft (4.74 m)
Surface speed	17.9 knots (33 km/h)
Submerged speed	8 knots (15 km/h)
Engine	Diesel engine generating 2,310 hp on the surface Electric engine generating 750 hp when submerged

ARMS & ARMOR

Torpedo tubes	Four in bow, one in stern, carrying fourteen torpedoes
Deck gun	3.5 in (88 mm) with 220 rounds

KMS *Tirpitz*

The German warship *Tirpitz* spent most of her brief career attacking Allied merchant ships in the Arctic Ocean.

The Norwegians called her the "Lonely Queen of the North" as she operated almost alone. She came into service on February 25, 1941, taking part in two missions against Allied convoys, with limited success. Her only battle was a bombardment of Svalbard (Spitzbergen Island) in the Arctic Ocean in September 1943.

FACT FILE

★ KMS *Tirpitz* and her sister ship KMS *Bismarck* were the only two ships of the Bismarck class, begun in 1936 and launched three years later. Germany hadn't built a battleship since World War I. They were in fact just bigger versions of World War I ships such as SMS *Seydlitz* (*see* pages 16–17).

★ In contrast to the *Tirpitz*, *Bismarck* sailed on only one mission. She sailed out into the North Atlantic on May 18, 1941, but was intercepted by a British fleet and sunk, on Prime Minister Winston Churchill's direct orders, on May 27th.

▼ *KMS* Tirpitz *was named after Grand Admiral Alfred von Tirpitz, who built up Germany's navy before World War I.*

SPECS & STATS

Launched Hamburg, Germany, April 1, 1939

Crew 2,608

Displacement 52,600 tons (53,442 t)

Length 823.8 ft (251 m)

Beam 118.2 ft (36 m)

Draft 28.6 ft (8.7 m)

Speed 30 knots (55 km/h)

Engines Twelve superheated boilers
Three 150,170 hp geared
steam turbines

▲ *Four of her powerful naval guns ready for action*

Almost Indestructible

The British regarded the *Tirpitz* as a huge threat to their shipping and made 10 attempts to destroy her while in port in Norway. The raids inflicted repeated damage but never sank the ship. By now, the *Tirpitz* was in no condition to go into action and was moved to a fjord west of Tromso. Here, two squadrons of Lancaster bombers eventually sank the ship on November 12, 1944, with three 5-ton (4.5-t) Tallboy bombs designed to penetrate heavily armored concrete buildings.

▼ *Aircraft were launched by hydraulic catapult.*

ARMS & ARMOR

Guns	Eight 15-in (380-mm) SKC 34 naval guns
	Twelve 5.9-in (150-mm) guns
	Sixteen 4.1-in (105-mm) guns
	Sixteen 1.46-in (37-mm) guns
	Ten 0.8-in (20-mm) guns
Torpedo tubes	Eight 21-in (533-mm) tubes
Aircraft	Four, with two catapults
Armor	Hull: up to 13 in (330 mm)

IJN *Yamato*

The Japanese warship IJN *Yamato* and her sister ship IJN *Musashi*, were the largest, heaviest battleships ever built.

▲ *A view of IJN* Yamato *at sea.*

Yamato's design was unique. Her deck rose and fell along the length of the hull, thus reducing weight. Her wide beam made her very stable, even in heavy seas. Her bulbous bow and partly flat stern reduced water resistance. Most importantly, her 18.1 in (460 mm) guns were the largest ever fitted to a battleship.

FACT FILE

★ In order to build this vast ship, the dry dock at Kure was deepened, the gantry crane strengthened, and part of the dock roofed over to prevent U.S. spies from observing its construction.

★ The main guns were so powerful that all the nearby antiaircraft gun positions on board were specially shielded to protect their gunners from the blast the main guns generated.

Battle History

Yamato saw service throughout the Pacific Ocean from 1942 to 1945, taking part in the assault on Midway Island in May/June 1942 and the Battle of the Philippine Sea in June 1944. Her final

Guns	Nine 18.1-in (460-mm) guns, Twelve 6.1-in (155-mm) guns Twelve 5-in (127-mm) guns, Twenty-four 1-in (25-mm) antiaircraft guns Four 0.5-in (13-mm) anti-aircraft guns
Aircraft	Seven reconnaissance aircraft, launched by two catapults
Armor	Hull: 16.1 in (410 mm) inclined at 20° Deck: 7.9 in (200 mm), Turrets: 25.6 in (650 mm)

SPECS & STATS

Launched	Kure, Japan, August 8, 1940
Crew	2,744
Displacement	71,650 tons (72,800 t)
Length	862.5 ft (263 m)
Beam	121 ft (36.9 m)
Draft	36 ft (11m)
Speed	27 knots (50 km/h)
Engines	Twelve boilers Four 150,000 hp steam turbines

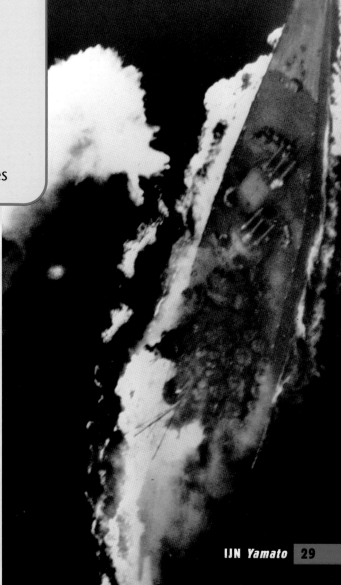

▼ *IJN* Yamato *sinks in April 1945.*

mission was Operation Ten-Go, following the U.S. invasion of Okinawa in April 1945. *Yamato* sailed out on April 6th to attack the U.S. fleet, which responded by sending 386 aircraft to intercept her and her nine escorts. She was hit by eight bombs and 12 torpedoes before capsizing and exploding. Of her crew, 2,475 men died, and only 269 survived.

Glossary

Anti-flash door
Strong, fireproof doors preventing the spread of fire to a ship's magazine.

Barbette
Armored cylinder for protecting the lower part of the turret of a warship.

Battery
Group of guns of the same size or used for the same purpose.

Battle cruiser
A warship with a battleship's armament but with the speed and maneuverability of a cruiser.

Battleship
Large, heavily armored warship with powerful guns.

Beam
Width of a ship.

Bulkhead
Wall-like partition inside the hull that strengthens the ship and keeps water from flowing along the length of the ship if the hull is breached.

Conning tower
Raised platform on a ship or submarine from which an officer can give directions to the helmsman.

Convoy
A group of ships sailing together for security.

Cruiser
High-speed, long-range warship of medium size.

Displacement
Weight of water moved out of the way by a ship when afloat and used to measure its weight.

Draft
Depth of a loaded ship or submarine in the water, taken from the waterline to the lowest point of the hull.

Elevator
Platform that carries aircraft from the hangar deck to the flight deck of an aircraft carrier.

Escort
To accompany a naval or merchant ship in order to protect it from enemy attack.

HMS/HMAS
His (or Her) Majesty's Ship. His (or Her) Majesty's Australian Ship.

hp
Horsepower, a unit of power.

Hull
Main body of a ship or submarine.

Hydraulic
Operated by pressure transmitted through a pipe by a liquid.

IJN
Imperial Japanese Navy.

KMS
Kriegsmarineschiff or "war navy ship."

Knot
1 nautical mile per hour = 1.15 mph (1.85 km/h).

Magazine
Part of a ship used for storing shells and other explosives.

pdr
Short for pounder; used to describe the weight of a shell.

Range
To aim a gun at a target.

Scuttle
To sink a ship deliberately.

SMU
Seiner Majestät Unterseeboot, "His Majesty's Submarine."

SMS
Seiner Majestät Schiff, "His Majesty's Ship."

Steam turbine
Turbine in which steam strikes blades and makes them turn to move the ship.

Torpedo
Underwater missile with an explosive warhead.

U-boat
German submarine; the "U" stands for *Unterseeboot,* "undersea boat."

USS
United States Ship.

Useful Web Sites

The Battleship Page—Museum Reference
http://www.battleship.org/html/Museums/Museums.htm

History of the U.S. Navy and Navy Ships
http://www.navyhistory.com/

History of the World's Navies
http://www.battleships-cruisers.co.uk/index.htm

The Imperial War Museum
http://www.iwm.org.uk/

Sites about the two World Wars:

The Great War (World War I) from PBS
www.pbs.org/greatwar/

The Perilous Fight: America's World War II in Color
www.pbs.org/perilousfight/battlefield/

BBC history sites about the two world wars:
www.bbc.co.uk/history/worldwars/wwone/
www.bbc.co.uk/history/worldwars/wwtwo/

Note to Parents and Teachers:
Every effort has been made by the publishers to ensure that the Web sites in this book are suitable for children, that they are of the highest educational value, and that they contain no inappropriate or offensive material. However, because of the nature of the Internet, it is impossible to guarantee that the contents of these sites will not be altered. We strongly advise that Internet access is supervised by a responsible adult.

Index